OTHER BOOKS OF SIMILAR INTEREST
FROM RANDOM HOUSE VALUE PUBLISHING

The Illustrated

Gettysburg Address

The Illustrated
Gettysburg
Address

R O B E R T A E . L A N D O N , EDITOR

GRAMERCY BOOKS
NEW YORK

This 2000 edition is published by Gramercy Books™, an imprint of Random House Value Publishing, Inc. 201 East 50th Street, New York, N.Y. 10022

Gramercy Books™ and design are trademarks of Random House Value Publishing, Inc.

Random House
New York • Toronto • London • Sydney • Auckland
http://www.randomhouse.com/

Printed and bound in the United States of America.

Designed by Karen Ocker

Library of Congress Cataloging–in–Publication Data

Lincoln, Abraham, 1809-1865.
  [Gettysburg address]
  The illustrated Gettysburg address / Roberta Landon.
    p. cm.
  ISBN 0-517-20749-4 (hc)
  1. Lincoln, Abraham, 1809-1865. Gettysburg address. 2. Lincoln, Abraham,
  1809-1865. Gettysburg address--Pictorial works. 3. United States--History--Civil War,
  1861-1865--Pictorial works. I. Landon, Roberta. II. Title.

  E475.55 .L74 2000
  974.7--dc21
                                                                99-056665

9 8 7 6 5 4 3 2 1

0-517-20749-4

On three very hot days in 1863, the town of Gettsyburg was the scene of the bloodiest battle in American history. When it was over, what began as a skirmish but ended as a full-scale battle involving more than 160,000 Americans. The town was left with more than 50,000 dead, wounded and ill. The more than 7,000 dead were put to rest in hastily dug graves or not buried at all.

Pennsylvania Governor Andrew Curtin was so distressed that he convinced David Wells, a Gettysburg attorney, to buy land for a proper burial ground for the Union dead. With the approval of the governor, Wills acquired 17 acres for the cemetery and hired a noted Pennsylvania landscape architect to draw a plan. On November 2, 1863, Wills invited President Lincoln to deliver a few remarks at the dedication ceremony.

On November 19, 1863, a crowd gathered at what is now the Gettysburg National Cemetery. The main speaker, Edward Everett of Massachusetts, a renowned orator who had been governor of Massachusetts, a member of both the U.S. House and Senate, U.S. Secretary of State and president of Harvard University, delivered a two-hour formal address. President Lincoln then spoke for just a few minutes. The speech was so short and was finished so quickly that the photographers missed it. Lincoln regarded the talk as a failure.

But these 272 words are now regarded as one of the finest American speeches—a masterpiece of American history. Everett wrote a note

★ ★ ★ ★ ★

to Lincoln on the day after the dedication: "I wish that I could flatter myself that I had come as near to the central idea of the occasion in two hours as you did in two minutes."

Historian Gary Wills has written:

"The crowd departed with a new thing in its ideological luggage, that new constitution Lincoln had substituted for the one they brought there with them. They walked off, from those curving graves on the hillside, under a changed sky, into a different America. Lincoln had revolutionized the Revolution, giving people a new past to live with that would change their future indefinitely."

Whether or not Lincoln realized the effect that this speech, or this war would have upon the union, we know today that without it, without the Emancipation Proclamation, and without the work that has brought our multiracial nation forward over the years, we would not, at the turn of the twenty-first century, be the same nation that we are today.

ROBERTA E. LANDON

Gettysburg Address

DELIVERED ON THE 19TH DAY OF NOVEMBER, 1863
CEMETERY HILL, GETTYSBURG, PENNSYLVANIA

..."the great American poem."

CARL SANDBURG

"...ceremony was rendered ludicrous by some of
the sallies of that poor President Lincoln."

CORRESPONDENT FROM LONDON

"...dishwatery, inane"

CHICAGO TIMES

"It is a model that will bear re-reading."

SPRINGFIELD, ILLINOIS NEWSPAPER

"The dedicatory remarks by President Lincoln
will live among the annals of man."

CHICAGO TRIBUNE

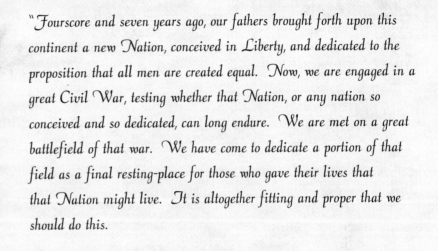

"Fourscore and seven years ago, our fathers brought forth upon this continent a new Nation, conceived in Liberty, and dedicated to the proposition that all men are created equal. Now, we are engaged in a great Civil War, testing whether that Nation, or any nation so conceived and so dedicated, can long endure. We are met on a great battlefield of that war. We have come to dedicate a portion of that field as a final resting-place for those who gave their lives that that Nation might live. It is altogether fitting and proper that we should do this.

But, in a larger sense, we cannot dedicate, we cannot consecrate, we cannot hallow this ground. The brave men, living and dead, who struggled here, have consecrated it far above our power to add or detract. The world will little note nor long remember what we say here, but it can never forget what they did here. It is for us, the living, rather to be dedicated to the great task remaining before us; that from these honored dead, we take increased devotion to that cause for which they gave the last full measure of devotion; that this Nation, under God, shall have a new birth of freedom; and that government of the People by the People and for the People shall not perish from the earth."

Abraham Lincoln

★　★　★　★　★

WILLS' INVITATION TO LINCOLN

Gettysburg Nov. 2 1863

To His Excellency

A. Lincoln

President U.S.

Sir,

The Several States having Soldiers in the Army of the Potomac, who were killed at the Battle of Gettysburg, or have since died at various hospitals which were established in the vicinity, have procured grounds on a prominent part of the Battle Field for a Cemetery, and are having the dead removed to them and properly buried.

These Grounds will be Consecrated and set apart to this Sacred purpose, by appropriate Ceremonies, on Thursday, the 19th instant. Hon Edward Everett will deliver the Oration.

I am authorized by the Governors of the different States to invite you to be present, and participate in these Ceremonies, which will doubtless be very imposing and solomnly impressive.

It is the desire that, after the Oration, you, as Chief Executive of the Nation, formally set apart these grounds to their Sacred use by a few appropriate remarks.

It will be a source of great gratification to the many widows and orphans that have been made almost friendless by the Great Battle here, to have you here personally; and it will kindle anew in the breasts of the Comrades of these brave dead, who are now in the tented field or nobly meeting the foe in the front, a confidence that they who sleep in death on the Battle Field are not forgotten by those highest in Authority; and they will feel that, should their fate be the same, their remains will not be uncared for.

We hope you will be able to be present to perform this last solemn act to the Soldiers dead on this Battle Field.

I am with great Respect, Your Excellency's Obedient Servant

David Wills Agent for A.G. Curtin Gov. of Penna. and acting for all the States

Gettysburg Nov. 2 1863
To His Excellency
A. Lincoln
President U.S.

Sir,
As the Hotels in our town will be crowded and in confusion at the time referred to in the enclosed invitation, I write to invite you to stop with me. I hope you will feel it your duty to lay aside pressing business for a day to come on here to perform this last sad rite to our brave Soldier dead on the 19th instant.

Governor Curtin and Hon Edwrd Everett will be my guests at that time and if you come you will please join them at my house.

You will confer a favor if you advise me early of your intentions.

With great Respect
Your Obedient Servant
David Wills

A bronzed lank man! His suit of ancient black

A famous high top-hat and plain worn shawl

Make him the quaint great figure that men love,

The prairie lawyer and master of us all.

VACHEL LINDSAY
("Abraham Lincoln Walks at Midnight")

"*Fourscore and seven years ago,*

★ ★ ★ ★ ★

JOHN BROWN'S RAID ON HARPER'S FERRY

JOHN BROWN and his entire family (which included 20 children) were involved in abolitionist work. On the evening of Sunday, October 16, 1859, John Brown and his men entered the town of Harpers Ferry, Virginia, took hostage some of its prominent citizens, and captured the federal arsenal. His intention, as he later made clear, was to liberate the slaves in the surrounding territory and form them into an army which would then fight to free all slaves.

For it is not John Brown the soldier that we praise; it is John Brown the moral hero; John Brown the noble confessor and martyr whom we honor, and whom we think it proper to honor in this day when men are carried away by the corrupt and pro-slavery clamor against him. Our weapons were drawn only from the armory of Truth; they were those of faith and hope and love. They were those of moral indignation strongly expressed against wrong. Robert Purvis has said that I was "the most belligerent non-resistant he ever saw." I accept the character he gives me; and I glory in it. I have no idea, because I am a non-resistant, of submitting tamely to injustice inflicted either on me or on the slave. I will oppose it with all the moral powers with which I am endowed.

LUCRETIA MOTT, remarks delivered at the 24th annual meeting of the Pennsylvania Anti-Slavery Society (October 25-26, 1860)

It is not merely for today, but for all time to come that we should perpetuate for our children's children this great free government which we have enjoyed all our lives.

ABRAHAM LINCOLN

our fathers brought forth

★ ★ ★ ★ ★

Any people anywhere, being inclined and having the power, have the
right to rise up and shake off the existing government and form one
that suits them better.

ABRAHAM LINCOLN

★ ★ ★ ★ ★

"On the morning of the raid, Monday, October 17, 1859, I was at my home near Shepherdstown (ten miles west of Harper's Ferry), and had hardly finished breakfast when a carriage came to the door with one of my daughters, who told me that a messenger had arrived at Shepherdstown, a few minutes before, with the starling intelligence of a negro insurrection at Harper's Ferry! ...Brown's actual force, all told, consisted of only twenty-two men including himself, three of whom never crossed the Potomac. Five of those who did cross were negroes, of whom three were fugitive slaves. Ten of them were killed in Virginia; seven were hanged there, and five are said to have escaped...Six of the white men were members of Brown's family, or connected with it by marriage, and five of these paid the forfeit of their lives to the Virginians. Owen Brown is the only one of the whole party who now survives....Between the time of his raid and his execution I saw Brown several times, and was sitting near him in the court-room when the sentence of death was pronounced upon him...Of course, I did not witness his execution, as I had seen quite enough of horrors at Harper's Ferry, little dreaming of those, ten thousand times more terrible, which I was yet to witness as among the results of the John Brown Raid."

RECOLLECTIONS OF ALEXANDER BOTELER, *CENTURY MAGAZINE*, (JULY 1883)

John brown (1800-1859)

"If John Brown did not end the war that ended slavery, he did, at least, begin the war that ended slavery. If we look over the dates, places, and men for which this honor is claimed, we shall find that not Carolina, but Virginia,—not Fort Sumter, but Harper's Ferry and the arsenal,-not Major Anderson, but John Brown began the war that ended American slavery, and made this a free republic. Until this blow was struck, the prospect for freedom was dim, shadowy, and uncertain. The irrepressible conflict was one of words, votes, and compromises. When John Brown stretched forth his arm the sky was cleared—the time for compromises was gone the armed hosts of freedom stood face to face over the chasm of a broken Union, and the clash of arms was at hand."

FREDERICK DOUGLASS, 1881 commencement, Storer College, at Harper's Ferry

upon this continent a new Nation,

THE EMANCIPATION PROCLAMATION

by the President of the United States of America: A Proclamation

Whereas on the 22nd day of September, (in the year of our Lord, one thousand eight hundred and sixty-two,) a proclamation was issued by the President of the United States, containing, among other things, the following, to wit:

"That on the 1st day of January, (in the year of our Lord, one thousand eight hundred and sixty-three,) all persons held as slaves within any State or designated part of a State the people whereof shall then be in rebellion against the United States shall be then, thenceforward, and forever free; and the executive government of the United States, including the military and naval authority thereof, will recognize and maintain the freedom of such persons and will do no act or acts to repress such persons, or any of them, in any efforts they may make for their actual freedom.

"That the executive will on the 1st day of January aforesaid, by proclamation, designate the States and parts of States, if any, in which the people thereof, respectively, shall then be in rebellion against the United States; and the fact that any State or the people thereof shall on that day be in good faith represented in the Congress of the United States by members chosen thereto at elections wherein a majority of the qualified voters of such States shall have participated shall, in the absence of strong countervailing testimony, be deemed conclusive evidence that such State and the people thereof are not then in rebellion against the United States."

Now, therefore, I, Abraham Lincoln, President of the United States, by virtue of the power in me vested as Commander-In-Chief of the Army and Navy of the United States in time of actual armed rebellion against the authority and government of the United States, and as a fit and necessary war measure for supressing said rebellion, do, on this 1st day of January, (in the year of our Lord, one thousand eight hundred and sixty-three,) and in accordance with my purpose so to do, publicly proclaimed for the full period of one hundred days from the first day above mentioned, order and designate as the States and parts of States wherein the people thereof, respectively, are this day in rebellion against the United States the following, to wit:

Arkansas, Texas, Louisiana (except the parishes of St. Bernard, Plaquemines, Jefferson, St. John, St. Charles, St. James, Ascension, Assumption, Terrebone, Lafourche, St. Mary, St. Martin, and Orleans, including the city of New Orleans), Mississippi, Alabama, Florida, Georgia, South Carolina, North Carolina, and Virginia (except the forty-eight counties designated as West Virginia, and also the counties of Berkley, Accomac, Morthhampton, Elizabeth City, York, Princess Anne, and Norfolk, including the cities of Norfolk and Portsmouth), and which excepted parts are for the present left precisely as if this proclamation were not issued.

And by virtue of the power and for the purpose aforesaid, I do order and declare that all persons held as slaves within said designated States and parts of States are, and henceforward shall be, free; and that the Executive Government of the United States, including the military and naval authorities thereof, will recognize and maintain the freedom of said persons.

And I hereby enjoin upon the people so declared to be free to abstain from all violence, unless in necessary self-defence; and I recommend to them that, in all case when allowed, they labor faithfully for reasonable wages.

And I further declare and make known that such persons of suitable condition will be received into the armed service of the United States to garrison forts, positions, stations, and other places, and to man vessels of all sorts in said service.

And upon this act, sincerely believed to be an act of justice, warranted by the Constitution upon military necessity, I invoke the considerate judgment of mankind and the gracious favor of Almighty God.

conceived in *Liberty,*

★ ★ ★ ★ ★

Whenever I hear anyone arguing
for slavery I feel a strong impulse
to see it tried on him personally.

ABRAHAM LINCOLN

ABRAHAM LINCOLN.

Gentlemen: I have, as you are aware, thought a great deal about the relation of this war to slavery...Several weeks ago, I read an order on this subject...which on account of objections made by some of you, was not issued. Ever since then my mind has been occupied with this subject...to issue a Proclamation of Emancipation. I said nothing to anyone but I made a promise to myself, and...to my Maker. I am going to fulfill that promise. I have got you together to hear what I have written down. I do not wish your advice about the main matter; for that I have determined for myself.

ABRAHAM LINCOLN addressing his Cabinet

MEN OF COLOR TO ARMS

MEN OF COLOR TO ARMS

"Who would be free themselves must strike the blow...I urge you to fly to arms and smite to death the power that would bury the Government and your liberty in the same hopeless grave. This is your golden opportunity."

FREDRICK DOUGLASS

In 1863, John Andrew, the War Governor of Massachusetts requested Secretary of War, Edwin Stanton, to create a volunteer regiment of African Americans. The Fifty-Fourth would include soldiers not only from Massachusetts but from all over the country. He called upon the help of Frederck Douglass and William Wells Brown. In just two months 1,000 men had enlisted in the volunteer army, with every state represented. The leader of this unit was Colonel Robert Shaw, not a black man.

Excellent Sir

My good friend says I must write to you and she will send it My son went in the 54th regiment. I am a colored woman and my son was strong and able as any to fight for his country and the colored people have as much to fight for as any. My father was a Slave and escaped from Louisiana before I was born morn forty year agoneI have but poor edication but I never went to schol, but I know just as well as any what is right between man and man. Now I know that it is right that a colored man should go and fight for his country, and so ought to a white man. I know that a colored man ought to run no greater risques that a white, his pay is no greater his obligation to fight is the same. So why should not our enemies be compelled to treat him the same, Made to do it.

Now Mr Lincoln dont you think you oght to stop this thing and make them do the same by the colored men....They tell me some do you will take back the Proclamation, don't do it. When you are dead and in Heaven, in a thousand years that action of yours will make the Angels sing your praises I know it.

Letter from the mother of a
Northern black soldier to President Lincoln

18

My Dear Wife it is with grate joy I take this time to let you know
Whare I am i am now in Safety in the 14th Regiment of Brooklyn
this Day i can Adress you thank god as a free man   I had a little tru-
ble in giting away But as the lord led the Children of Isrel to the
land of Canon So he led me to a land Whare fredom Will rain in
spite Of earth and hell…..

JOHN BOSTON, Virginia, January 12, 1862

No man is good enough to govern another
man without that other's consent.

ABRAHAM LINCOLN

As I would not be a *slave* so I would not be a *master.*

ABRAHAM LINCOLN

When I see strong hands sowing, reaping, and
threshing wheat into bread, I cannot refrain from wishing
and believing that those hands, some way in God's
good time, shall own the mouth they feed.

ABRAHAM LINCOLN

and ***dedicated*** *to the* ***proposition*** ★ ★ ★ ★

Fellow-citizens, we cannot escape history. We of this Congress and this administration, will be remembered in spite of ourselves. No personal significance, or insignificance, can spare one or another of us. The fiery trial through which we pass, will light us down, in honor or dishonor, to the latest generation. We say we are for the Union. The world will not forget that we say this. We know how to save the Union. The world knows we do know how to save it. We—even we here—hold the power, and bear the responsibility.

In giving freedom to the slave, we assure freedom to the free—honorable alike in what we give, and what we preserve. We shall nobly save, or meanly lose, the last best hope of earth. Other means may succeed; this could not fail. The way is plain, peaceful, generous, just—a way which, if followed, the world will forever applaud, and God must forever bless.

ABRAHAM LINCOLN'S ANNUAL MESSAGE TO CONGRESS (December 3, 1862)

To you, white man, the world throws wide her gates; the way is clear to wealth, to fame, to glory, to renown; the high places of independence and honor and trust are yours; all your efforts are praised and encouraged; all your successes are welcomed with loud hurrah and cheers; but the black man and the woman are born to shame. The badge of degredation is the skin and the sex....For while the man is born to do whatever he can, for the woman and the negro there is no such privilege.

ELIZABETH CADY STANTON (*The Liberator*, May 1860)

Have we not a right here? For 300 years or more, we have had a foothold on this continent. We have grown up with you. We levelled your forests, Our hands removed the stumps from your fields and raised the first crops and brought the first produced to your tables. We have fought for this country....I consider it settled that the black and white people of America ought to share common destiny. The white and black must fall or flourish together. We have been with you, are still with you, and mean to be with you to the end. We shall neither die out nor be driven out. But we shall go with you and stand either as a testimony against you or as evidence in your favor throughout all your generations.

FREDERICK DOUGLASS (1851)

What, to the American slave, is your 4th of July? I answer: a day that reveals to him, more than all other days in the year, the gross injustice and cruelty to which he is the constant victim.

FREDRICK DOUGLASS

that all men are created equal. ★ ★ ★ ★ ★

When Grant once gets possession of a place, he holds onto it as if he had inherited it.

ABRAHAM LINCOLN, 1864

I can't spare this man—he fights.

ABRAHAM LINCOLN

It is the dogged pertinacity of Grant that wins.

ABRAHAM LINCOLN

The man of all men who knew General Grant best, his friend and chief ally, General W. T. Sherman, declared that Grant more nearly than any other man impersonated the American character of 1861-1865, and was the typical hero of our great Civil War.

It is an anomaly of history that a man so distinguished in war should be so unwarlike in personal characteristics as was Ulysses Simpson Grant, and so singularly free from the ambitions supposed to dominate the soldier.

"Sam" Grant, as his colleagues at the Military Academy were accustomed to call him, because of the "U.S.," Uncle Sam in his name; " 'Sam Grant," as one of those same colleagues once said, "was as honest a man as God ever made..."

It was characteristic of Grant's mental processes that he always thought on straight lines, and his action was equally direct and positive. He was not so much concerned with the subtleties of strategy as with a study of the most direct road to the opponent's center. One of the chief perplexities on the field of battle is "the fog of war," the difficulty of divining the movements of the foe, by which your own are to be determined. Grant was less confused by this than most commanders, keeping his adversary so occupied with his own aggressive movements that he had little opportunity to study combinations against him.

WILLIAM CONANT CHURCH, Brevet Lieutenant-Colonel,
United States Volunteers

His soldiers always knew that he was ready to rough it with them and share their hardships on the march. He wore no better clothes than they, and often ate no better food.

HORACE PORTER, *Campaigning with General Grant*

My…experience has taught me two lessons: first, that things are seen plainer after the events have occurred; second, that the most confident critics are generally those who know the least about the matter criticized.

U. S. GRANT in *The Personal Memoirs of Ulysses S. Grant*

They [the troops] remembered, once, how Grant tried to ride past the marching column, found that his horse was spattering the soldiers with mud, and left the road to pick his way through the underbrush not returning to the road until he had reached the head of the column. An Ohio private recalled that the men were ready to cheer him for his considerate act, and wrote that the little incident "shows the kind of man on whose shoulders the greatest responsibilities were to be placed."

CHARLES W. WRIGHT, *A Corporal's Story: Experiences in the Ranks of Company c, 81st Ohio Volunteer Infantry*

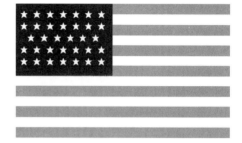

Now, we are engaged

He's the quietest little fellow you ever saw. The only evidence you have that he's in any place is that he makes things git. Wherever he is, things move.

ABRAHAM LINCOLN

23

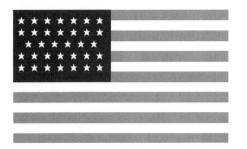

It was a place which I had never seen in my life, and had no more knowledge of than you have now. Yet it would seem that a glance at a map should have revealed its importance. This little town occupies, as it were, the hub of a wheel, from which roads, or spokes, radiate in every direction: northwestward toward Chamberburg; northeastward toward Harrisburg and Philadelphia; southwestward toward the Potomac; souteastward toward Baltimore. Whosoever held Gettysburg, held, if he knew it, the key to a campaign.

UNION GENERAL GEORGE G. MEAD to Congressional Committee on the Conduct of the War

COMMUNICATION BETWEEN MEADE AND HALLECK

HALLECK: I need hardly say to you that the escape of Lee's army without another battle has created great dissatisfactionin the mind of the President, and it will require an active and energetic pursuit on your part to remove the impression that it has nobeen sufficiently active heretofore.

MEADE: Having performed my duty conscientiously and to the best of my ability, the censure of the President is in my judgment so undeserved that I feel compelled most respectfully to ask to be immediately relieved from the command of this army.

HALLECK: My telegram stating the disappointment of the President at the escape of Lee's army was not intended as a censure, but as a stimulus to an active pursuit. It is not deemed a sufficient cause for your application to be relieved.

Your golden opportunity is lost. A good consummation
was within your easy reach but you let it slip.

ABRAHAM LINCOLN
to Meade after Gettysburg

in a great

Civil War, ★ ★ ★ ★

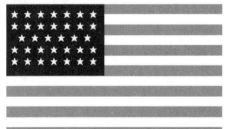

LINCOLN TO MAJOR GENERAL JOSEPH HOOKER

You have confidence in yourself, which is a valuable, if not an indispensable quality. You are ambitious, which within reasonable bounds does good rather than harm.

He is an admirable engineer, [McClellan] but he seems to have a special talent for the stationary engine.

ABRAHAM LINCOLN

LINCOLN TO MAJOR GENERAL HENRY HALLECK

Have you a plan? If you have one, prosecute without interference from me. If you have not, please inform me so that I can try to assist in the formation of one.

If at any time you [McClellan] feel able to—take the offensive. You are not restrained from doing so.

ABRAHAM LINCOLN

He [Sheridan] is one of those long-armed fellows with short legs that can scratch his shins without having to stoop over to do so.

ABRAHAM LINCOLN

Philip Henry Sheridan

Beware of rashness, but with energy and sleepless vigilance go forward and give us victories.

GEORGE B. MCCLELLAN, Union Army General, Commander of the Army of the Potomac

Henry Wagner Halleck

George Brinton McClellan

Hoseph Hooker

John F. Reynolds

I will hold McClellan's horse if he will only bring success.

ABRAHAM LINCOLN

testing whether that Nation, ★ ★ ★ ★

It had not been intended to deliver a general battle so far from our base unless attacked, but coming unexpectedly upon the whole Federal army, to withdraw through the mountains with our extensive trains would have been difficult and dangerous. At the same time we were unable to await an attack, as the country was unfavorable for collecting supplies in the presence of the enemy, who could restrain our foraging parties by holding the passes with local and other troops. A battle had, therefore, become in a measure unavoidable, and the success already gained gave hope of a favorable issue.

From report of ROBERT E. LEE, The Gettsyburg Campaign (June 3 to August 1, 1863. Submitted June 7, 1864)

Raised by his mother, Anne Carter Lee, Robert E. Lee entered West Point in 1825. He graduated second in his class and spent the next 15 years in the elite Corps of Engineers. After serving in the Mexican War, he returned to West Point as superintendent in 1852.

In 1861, Lee was offered command of the Union army. Although opposed to both secession and slavery, Lee could not agree to fight against his home state of Virginia. "I cannot raise my hand against my birthplace, my home, my children.... Whatever may be the result of the contest I foresee that the county will have to pass through a terrible ordeal, a necessary expiation for our national sin."

★ ★ ★ ★ ★ *or any nation*

I would have much preferred, had your choice fallen upon an abler man. Trusting in Almighty God, an approving conscience, and the aid of my fellow-citizens, I devote myself to the service of my native State, in whose behalf alone, will I ever again draw my sword.

MAJOR-GENERAL LEE at his appointment as
Commander-in-chief of Virginia forces at Virginia Convention (1861)

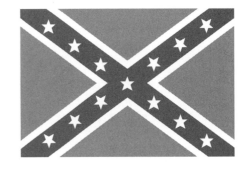

Our people must rest quiet upon the fact that the military preparations, for our defence, are under the direction of shrewd, skilful, indefatigable, experienced, and patriotic officers. Our commanding general, Robert E. Lee, has long been the pride of the service, and he is supported by subordinates of acknowledged capacity and large experience.

VIRGINIA NEWSPAPER, (1861)

Never mind, General, all this has been *my* fault; it is *I* that have lost this fight, and you must help me out of it in the best way you can.

ROBERT E. LEE to General Wilcox, on July 3, 1863.

"General Lee has been the only great man with whom I have been thrown who has not dwindled upon a near approach."

MAJOR A. R. H. RANSOM of the Confederate artillery

...of all the great figures in history and literature whom he has had occasion to study through books, no one has stood out freer from human imperfections, of whatever sort, than the man and soldier upon whom were centered the affections, the admiration, and the-hopes of the Southern people during the great crisis in their history.

WILLIAM P. TENT, Professor of English Literature in Columbia University

This has been a sad day for us, Colonel, a sad day; but we can't expect always to gain victories.

ROBERT E. LEE to Col. Fremantle, British Army, on July 3, 1863

Up men, to your posts! Don't forget today that you are from Old Virginia.

GEN. GEORGE E. PICKETT to his troops before the ill-fated charge on July 3, 1863

The behavior of my troops throughout this campaign was beyond praise, whether the points considered be their alacrity and willing endurance of the long marches, their orderly and exemplary conduct in the enemy's country, their bravery in action, or their patient endurance of hunger, fatigue and exposure during our retreat.

The lists of killed and wounded, as well as the result gained, will show the desperate character of their fighting.

R. S. EWELL, Lieutenant General, Provisional Army, CSA on the Gettysburg Campaign (August 1863)

A.P. Hill

…There is little to record of General Hill that has not already been stated…His individuality is merged in the glorious deeds of the army wherein he bore so high and important a position. To relate, in detail, what was done by this brave and skilful officer at Chancellorsville, and again in Maryland and Pennsylvania, would involve useless repetition…

CAPTAIN WILLIAM P. SNOW, *Lee and His Generals*

"I could now," says [Colonel] Fremantle, "thoroughly appreciate the term bull-dog, which I had heard applied to him [Longstreet]by his soldiers. Difficulties seemed to make no other impression upon him than to make him a little more savage."

CAPTAIN WILLIAM P. SNOW, *Lee and His Generals*

James Longstreet

so conceived and so dedicated,

About 1 P.M. , at a given signal, a heavy cannonade was opened, and continued for about two hours with marked effect upon the enemy. His batteries replied vigorously at first, but toward the close their fire slackened perceptibly, and General Longstreet ordered forward the column of attack, consisting of Pickett's and Heath's divisions, in two lines, Pickett on the right. Wilcox's brigade marched in rear of Pickett's right, to guard that flank, and Heth's was supported by Lane's and Scales' brigades under General Trimble.

The troops moved steadily on, under a heavy fire of musketry and artillery, the main attack being directed against the enemy's left center.

His batteries reopened as soon as they appeared. Our own having nearly exhausted their ammunition in the protracted cannonade that preceded the advance of the infantry, were unable to reply or render the necessary support to the attacking party. Owing to this fact, which was unknown to me when the assault took place, the enemy was enabled to throw a strong force of infantry against our left, already waving under a concentrated fire of artillery from the ridge in front, and from Cemetery Hill, on the left. It finally gave way, and the right, after penetrating the enemy's lines, entering his advance works and capturing some of his artillery, was attacked simultaneously in front and on both flanks and driven back with heavy loss.

The troops were rallied and reformed, but the enemy did not pursue.

From report of ROBERT E. LEE, The Gettsyburg Campaign
(June 3 to August 1, 1863. Submitted June 7, 1864)

J.E.B. Stuart

JAMES EWELL BROWN ("JEB") STUART, who with his colorful uniform, piercing eyes and ruddy complexion, would at first be taken as "a daring chief of some wild predatory band," was the Confederate army's best cavalry commander. A graduate of West Point, Stuart resigned from the U.S. Army in 1861 and returned to Virginia. His skills led him to be named lieutenant colonel, then captain and finally brigadier general. With successful raids at Bill Run, Antietam, Fredericksburg and Chancellorsville, Stuart—on a scouting mission to prepare for Gettysburg—missed the first day of battle and arrived on the second day to witness the Confederate defeat.

"As I often stood in the quiet Evergreen Cemetery, when we knew naught but the smiles of Peace, gazing to the distant South Mountains, or the nearer Round Tops, or Culp's Hill, little did I dream that from those summits the engines of war would, in a few years, belch forth their missiles of destruction; that through those sylvan aisles would reverberate the clash of arms, the roar of musketry, and the booming of cannon, to be followed by the groans of the wounded and dying.

can long endure.

★ ★ ★ ★ ★

Little did I think that those lovely valleys teeming with verdure and the rich harvest, would soon be strewn with the distorted and mangled bodies of American brothers; making a rich ingathering for the grim monster Death; that across that peaceful lane would charge the brave and daring "Louisiana Tigers," thirsting for their brother's blood, but soon to be hurled back filling the space over which they advanced with their shattered and dead bodies.

TILLIE (PIERCE) ALLEMAN, *At Gettysburg*, or *What A Girl Saw and Heard of the Battle, A True Narrative.* (1888)

War council of General Meade before the battle of Gettysburg.

"As for myself, I had scarcely reached the front door, when, on looking up the street, I saw some of the men on horseback. I scrambled in, slammed shut the door, and hastening to the sitting room, peeped out between the shutters.

What a horrible sight! There they were, human beings! Clad almost in rags, covered with dust, riding wildly, pell-mell down the hill toward our home! Shouting, yelling, most unearthly, cursing brandishing their revolvers, and firing right and left."

TILLIE (PIERCE) ALLEMAN, *At Gettysburg*

Union cavalry photographed at Gettysburg.

"It was not long after our arrival, until Union artillery came hurrying by. It was indeed a thrilling sight. How the men impelled their horses! How the officers urged the men as they all flew past toward the sound of the battle! Now the road is getting all cut up; they take to the field, and all is an anxious, eager hurry! Shouting, lashing the horses, cheering the men, they all rush madly on."

TILLIE (PIERCE) ALLEMAN, *At Gettysburg*

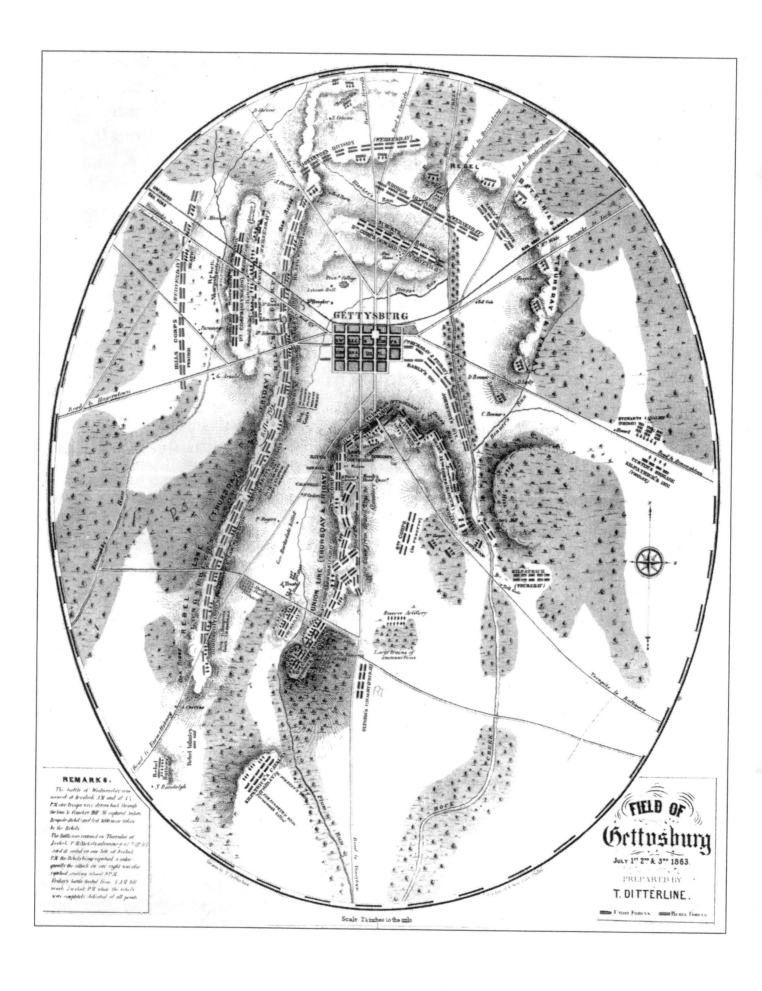

FIELD OF Gettysburg

JULY 1ST 2ND & 3RD 1863.

PREPARED BY

T. DITTERLINE.

Scale 2½ inches to the mile

Union Forces ▬▬▬ Rebel Forces ▬▬▬

★ ★ ★ ★ ★

on a great battlefield of that war.

★ ★ ★ ★

 In June of 1863, General Robert E. Lee decided to take the war north, hoping to attack Philadelphia, Baltimore, and Washington. Confederate troops were spread through southern Pennsylvania when Union troops were spotted in Gettysburg.

"As we drove along in the cool of the evening, we noticed that everywhere confusion prevailed. Fences were thrown down near and far; knapsacks, blankets and many other articles, lay scattered here and there. The whole country seemed filled with desolation.

Upon reaching the place I fairly shrank back aghast at the awful sight presented. The approaches were crowded with wounded, dying and dead. The air was filled with moanings and groanings. As we passed on toward the house, we were compelled to pick our steps in order that we might not tread on the prostrate bodies.

TILLIE (PIERCE) ALLEMAN, *At Gettysburg*

★ ★ ★ ★

"Either the opponents of slavery will arrest the further spread of it, and place it where the public mind shall rest in the belief that it is in course of ultimate extinction; or its advocates will push it forward, till it shall become alike lawful in all the States, old as well as new— North as well as South."

From LINCOLN'S famous "House Divided" speech (July 1, 1858)

We have come

★ ★ ★ ★

★ ★ ★ ★ ★

GETTYSBURG

To do and dare, and die at need,
But while life lasts, to fight—
For right or wrong a simple creed,
But simplest for the right.

They faltered not who stood that day
And held this post of dread;
Nor cowards they who wore the gray
Until the gray was red.

JAMES JEFFREY ROCHE (July 2nd, 1892)

 The Battle of Gettysburg began on July 1, when Confederate troops attacked Union cavalry. Union forces were outnumbered, but managed to hold until afternoon, when they were overpowered by southern troops.

Death of General F. Reynolds on July 1, 1863

[I will] "throw an overwhelming force on their advance, crush it, follow up the success, drive one corps back on another, and by successive repulses and surprises...create a panic and virtually destroy the army...The war will be over and we shall achieve the recognition of our independence."

ROBERT E. LEE on July 2, 1863

to dedicate a portion of that field

This war is eating my life out.

ABRAHAM LINCOLN

THE HIGH TIDE AT GETTYSBURG

A cloud possessed the hollow field,

The gathering battle's smoky shield:

    Athwart the gloom the lightning flashed,

    And through the cloud some horsemen dashed,

And from the heights the thunder pealed.

Then, at the brief command of Lee,

Moved out that matchless infantry,

    With Pickett leading grandly down,

    To rush against the Roaring crown

Of those dread heights of destiny.

WILL HENRY THOMPSON

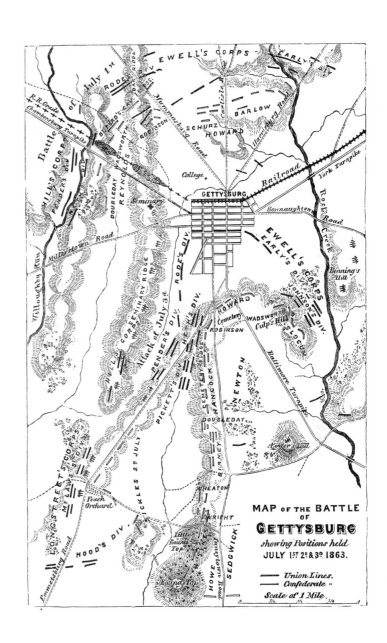

MAP OF THE BATTLE OF GETTYSBURG
showing Positions held
JULY 1ST 2D & 3D 1863.

—— Union Lines.
—— Confederate "
Scale of 1 Mile.

as a final resting-place

★ ★ ★ ★

Diary of Samuel Cormany
July 2, 1863

Thursday. More or less Picket firing all night—We were aroused early, and inspection showed a lot of our horses too lame and used up for good action—So first, our good mounts were formed for moving out, and we were soon off—with the Brigade and took Reb. Genl. Steward by surprise on the Deardorf Farm...Towards noon firing became more general and in almost all directions—and we were ordered to our horses—and joined our returned heroes, and lay in readiness for any emergency—The general battle increaced in energy—and occasional fierceness—and by 2 P.M. the canonading was most terrific and continued til 5 P.M. and was interspersed with musketry—and Charge—yells everything that goes to making up the indescribable battle of the best men on Earth, seemingly in the Fight to the Finish—At dark, our Cav Bri—2nd Brig 2" Div—was moved to the left—many wounded came in—Taken as a whole from all one can see from one point—it seems as tho our men—The Union Army—is rather overpowered and worsted...

 On July 2, battle lines were drawn a mile apart on two parallel ridges. Lee attacked both flanks of the famous Union "fish hook." The Union army proved difficult to undermine and poor communication kept the Confederacy from winning.

for those who
gave their lives that

★ ★ ★ ★ ★

Confederate attack on Culp Hill, July 3rd

ACCOUNT FROM SOLDIER THEODORE GERRISH ON 2ND DAY OF BATTLE OF GETTYSBURG

With a cheer and a flash of his [Colonel Joshua Chamberlain] sword, that sent inspiration along the line, full ten pages to the front he sprang..."Come on! Come on, boys!" he shouts. The colour segeant and the brave colour guard follow, and with one wild yell of anguish wrung from its tortured heart, the regiment charged.

The rebels were confounded by the movement. We struck them with a fearful shock. They recoil, stagger, break and run, and like avenging demons our men pursue. The rebels rush towards a stone wall...A band of our men leap over the wall and capture at least a hundred prisoners.

that Nation might live.

Have you heard the story that gossips tell
Of Burns of Gettsyburg? No? Ah, well:
Brief is the glory that hero earns,
Briefer the story of poor John Burns:
He was the fellow who won renown,—
The only man who didn't back down
When the rebels rode through his native town;

But held his own in the fight next day,
When all his townsfolk ran away.
That was in July, sixty-three,—
The very day that General Lee,
Flower of Southern chivalry,
Baffled and beaten, backward reeled
From a stubborn Meade and a barren field.

FRANCIS BRET HARTE, John Burns of Gettysburg

A few days after the battle…"I stood on Cemetery Hill, and, looking westward, the Dobbin homestead lay before me, the old stone house….defaced with shot and shell, with devastation all around it."

HIRAM WERTZ

 On July 3, Lee decided to attack the union center on Cemetery Ridge. In the afternoon, after struggling in a duel against Union forces, a massive infantry of 15,000 Confederate troops led by General George E. Pickett, began their assault on the Union center. They failed to break the Union line, and in less than one hour, 10,000 Confederate soldiers had become casualties. This attack, known as Pickett's Charge, was the failure that ended the battle. General George C. Meade, commander of the Union Army of the Potomac, had kept the Confederate army at bay in what was to be known as the greatest battle of the Civil War.

"The National Cemetery, wherein repose the heroic dead, has become a marvel of loveliness. Baptized with the blood of patriots, dedicated in the immortal words of Lincoln nurtured and guarded by a grateful people, this spot for all time to come cannot be other than the nation's shrine of American virtue, valor and freedom."

TILLIE (PIERCE) ALLEMAN, *At Gettysburg*

If destruction be our lot we must ourselves
be its author and finisher. As a nation of freemen
we must live through all time, or die by suicide.

ABRAHAM LINCOLN

It is altogether fitting

★ ★ ★ ★ ★

and proper that we should do this.

★ ★ ★ ★ ★

DIARY OF SAMUEL CORMANY

JULY 3, 1863

Friday. Canonading commenced early—and battle was on again in full intensity at 10 ock we were ordered to the Front and Center....From 1-1/2 til 4 P.M. there was the heaviest canonading I ever have heard....Our Boys opened 54 guns at the same time on the Rebel lines and works from a little conical hill, Cemetary Ridge. We were picketing in the rear and on the right of it—Many shells came our way—some really quite near—But it is wonderful how few really made our acquaintance.

"By this time the Union dead had been principally carried off the field and those that remained were Confederates.

As we stood upon those might bowlders, and looked down into the chasms between, we beheld the dead lying there just as they had fallen during the struggle. From the summit of Little Round Top, surrounded by the wrecks of battle, we gazed upon the valley of death beneath. The view there spread out before us was terrible to contemplate! It was an awful spectacle! Dead soldiers, bloated horses, shattered cannon and caissons, thousands of small arms. In fact everything belonging to army equipments, was there in one confused and indescribable mass."

TILLIE (PIERCE) ALLEMAN, *At Gettysburg*

 When the battle ended, the town of Gettysburg, with a population of 2,400 was left with more than 51,000 casualties. More than 172,000 men and 634 cannon had been positioned in an area encompassing 25 square miles.

"Angle" Lewis Armistad destroys Union battery.

But, in a larger sense,

★ ★ ★ ★ ★

The dogmas of the quiet past are inadequate to the stormy present.
The occasion is piled high with difficulty, and we must rise with the
occasion. As our case is new so we must think anew and act anew.
We must disenthrall ourselves, and then we shall save our children.

ABRAHAM LINCOLN

Wreckage of Union battery before Pickett's charge.

Dear are the dead we weep for;

Dear are the strong hearts broken!

Proudly their memory we keep for

Our help and hope; a token

Of sacred thought too deep for

Words that leave it unspoken.

All that we know of fairest,

All that we have of meetest,

Here we lay down for the rarest

Doers whose souls rose fleetest,

And in their homes of air rest,

Ranked with the truest and sweetest.''

GEORGE PARSONS LATHROP, *Gettysburg: A Battle Ode Read*

at the reunion of Confederate soldiers, (July 3, 1888)

we cannot *dedicate,* ★ ★ ★ ★ ★

★ ★ ★ ★ ★

DIARY OF SAMUEL CORMANY

JULY 4, 1863

Saturday. The great battle closed and quieted with the closing day—Some firing at various points—

...We had fed, eaten, and were standing "to horse" when about 6 ock NEWS CAME—"The Rebs are falling back!" and "Our Forces are following them" and our Regt went out towards Hunterstown reconnoitering....we were ordered to camp near Hanover—where we first lay on arriving near Gettysburg—Evening awfully muddy and disagreeable—I saw much of the destructiveness of the Johnies today—

Body of a Confederate soldier at the foot of Little Round Top, Gettysburg.

DIARY OF SAMUEL CORMANY

JULY 5, 1863

Sunday. Rained awfully during the night. I got very wet—

Early we took up the march for Chambersburg—Crossing the battlefield—Cemitary Hill—The Great Wheat Field Farm, Seminary ridge—and other places where dead men, horses, smashed artillery, were strewn in utter confusion, the Blue and The Grey mixed—Their bodies so bloated—distorted—discolored on account of decomposition having set in—that they were utterly unrecognizable, save by clothing, or things in their pockets—The scene simply beggars description...

we cannot consecrate,

★ ★ ★ ★ ★

Mine eyes have seen the glory of the coming of the Lord:

He is trampling out the vintage where the grapes of wrath are stored;

He hath loosed the fateful lightning of his terrible swift sword:

His truth is marching on.

JULIA WARD HOWE, Battle-Hymn of The Republic (1861)

LITTLE GIFFIN

Out of the focal and foremost fire,
Out of the hospital walls as dire,
Smitten of grapeshot and gangrene
(Eighteenth battle, and he sixteen!),
Specter such as we seldom see,
Little Giffin of Tennessee!

DR. FRANCIS O. TICKNOR

Both sides took prisoners, but from all the information we could get we got several thousand more than we lost. All in all, the battle of Gettysburg was the grandest fight of the war. Our men never fought better and the rebels never were more desperate. The result is a repulsed and discomfited enemy.

It is true many gallant officers and brave men have fallen in this battle. It is true that our town and county has suffered terribly. It is true that houses and barns have been burned—fences torn down and crops destroyed all over the country—and yet we have much to be thankful for. The invader has been driven from our state, severely punished for his temerity, and we can once more breathe freely. The brave Army of the Potomac deserves and will receive our heartfelt thanks, our everlasting gratitude.

GETTYSBURG COMPILER, (July 1863)

Our usually quiet and unpretending little town of Gettysburg has become historic. During the last two weeks, scenes have been enacted here that beggar all description. War has been raging all around us in its most horrid form. Two mighty armies have passed through our county and the bloodiest fight of the war has taken place in our midst.

For some time past it has been evident that a great battle must come off in our state, and perhaps in or near our county, but no one supposed that Gettysburg would be the place selected.

GETTYSBURG COMPILER, (July 1863)

we cannot hallow this ground. ★ ★ ★ ★

★ ★ ★ ★ ★

LETTER FROM JOSEPH THEOBALD GERBRON, A SILVER ENGRAVER FROM PHILADELPHIA,
FROM A HOSPITAL AFTER BEING WOUNDED AT SNICKER'S FORD, JULY 18, 1864

I was almost led to believe there was no fighting there at all but Comrad Bogardus has relieved my mind some of that point. As near as I can remember we crossed the river on the morning of the 18th. I got in a feed trough back of a wagon so I did not get wet.

We marched in line of battle under a heavy fire across the field to a stone fence where we made a stand. I was wounded there and in re-crossing the river I saw several shot—one belonging to 1st W. Va. and one who was helping me was shot. I tried to help him out but left him on the bank as near as I can remember. The 54th Pa. And 11th and 15th W. Va. were in the same Brigade and anyone who says there was no fighting there was not there or was hiding in the bushes....

The brave men,

★ ★ ★ ★ ★

Mrs. Bixby, Boston, Massachusetts.

Dear Madam: I have been shown in the files of the War Department a statement of the Adjutant-General of Massachusetts that you are the mother of five sons who have died gloriously in the field of battle. I feel how weak and fruitless must be any words of mine which should attempt to beguile you from the grief of a loss so overwhelming. But I cannot refrain from tendering to you the consolation that may be found in the thanks of the Republic they died to save. I pray that our heavenly Father may assuage the anguish of your bereavement, and leave you only the cherished memory of the loved and lost, and the solemn pride that must be yours to have laid so costly a sacrifice upon the altar of freedom.

Yours very sincerely and respectfully,

Abraham Lincoln

(November 21, 1864)

★ ★ ★ ★ ★

living and *dead*,

★ ★ ★ ★ ★

★ ★ ★ ★ ★

★ ★ ★ ★

who struggled here,

I saw the battle-corpses, myriads of them,

And the white skeletons of young men, I saw them,

I saw the débris and débris of all the slain soldiers of the war,

But I saw they were not as was thought,

They themselves were fully at rest, they suffer'd not,

The living man remain'd and suffer'd, the mother suffer'd,

And the wife and the child and the musing comrade suffer'd,

And the armies that remain'd suffer'd

WALT WHITMAN, FROM
"WHEN LILACS LAST IN HE DOORYARD BLOOM'D"

have **consecrated it**

★ ★ ★ ★ ★

My dear Pa and Ma,

How shall I prepare you for the sad and heart-rending tidings? Our family, heretofore so fortunate during this struggle, must now mourn the loss of a "loved one": Brother Jester is no more. He now "sleeps the sleep that knows no waking," beneath Georgia's bloodstained soil, a glorious martyr to the cause of liberty. He was killed near Marietta, Georgia, June 22, while on skirmish… At the beginning of the third charge he was wounded slightly, but he would not retire from the field, and as our skirmishers were balling back, the "Yanks" pursuing them, he stopped and turned to look back—just as he turned, the fatal ball popped through his chest, killing him almost instantly…"

Your Son, Affectionately,
Milton [Walls]
25th Regt. Ark. Vols.
D. H. Reynolds Brg. Walthal Division,
Stewart Corps Army of Tenn. (August 1864)

far above our power

THE NATIONAL TRIBUNE, OCTOBER 20, 1887 ON THE BATTLE OF SPOTTSYLVANIA

On the 7th of May, 1864, the 126th Ohio lay in line of battle a short distance to the left of where it suffered so severely the day previously in the Battle of the Wilderness. The regiment crossed the Rapidan three days before with 23 officers and 555 men—all strong and able for duty. But now its number was reduced nearly one-half in slain, wounded and missing....Shortly after nightfall the regiment, with its division—Third Division, Sixth Corps, withdrew quietly from the rebel front and began its march with the entire army in the direction of Spottsylvania Courthouse, on what is known as the Brock Road. The regiment was on the go all night. When not marching, the men were standing on their feet impatiently waiting which was as tiresome and fatiguing as the marching, as they were not allowed in any way to relieve themselves of their burden. This slow and tiresome march was kept up till nearly evening of the next day—Sunday.

JOHN E. PECK, CAPTAIN, 126TH OHIO, JEWETT, OHIO

to *add* or *detract.*

★ ★ ★ ★ ★

...Now the regiment was very small, only a remnant, not enough for a company of minimum size, and a sense of loneliness seemed to come over the men that night as they lay in line of battle thinking of so many comrades sleeping the sleep of death only a short distance from them. ...The battle continued through the night and until 3 o'clock the next morning, when Lee withdrew his shattered columns to new works that he had erected nearly a mile in rear. At daylight the Union advanced and took possession of the rebel works. In front of where the 126th fought the day before, what a horrifying sight in the advanced rifle-pits! Lee, in retiring, had left his dead and wounded, and here they were piled by the hundreds. Such a sight will never be forgotten by those who saw it. Bloated corpses and men in the agonies of death; the dead and dying lay piled upon each other, the ditch red with human gore; trees in rear of the rifle pits were actually hacked down by bullets and had fallen on the slain and wounded as they lay all around. Language fails to describe the scene, and I drop the curtain...

JOHN E. PECK, CAPTAIN, 126th Ohio, Jewett, Ohio

The world will little note

★ ★ ★ ★ ★

★ ★ ★ ★ ★

THE FADED COAT OF BLUE
J.H. McNAUGHTON

My brave lad he sleeps in his faded coat of blue;

In a lonely grave unknown lies the heart that beat so true;

He sank faint and hungry among the famished brave,

And they laid him sad and lonely within his nameless grave.

Chorus:

No more bugle calls the weary one,

Rest noble spirit, in thy grave unknown!

I'll find you and know you, among the good and true,

When a robe of white is giv'n for the faded coat of blue.

nor long remember

★ ★ ★ ★

★ ★ ★ ★

what we say here,

★ ★ ★ ★

★ ★ ★ ★ ★

With malice toward none, with charity for all, with firmness in the right as God gives us to see the right, let us strive on to finish the work we are in, to bind up the nation's wounds, to care for him who shall have borne the battle and for his widow and his orphan, to do all which may achieve and cherish a just and lasting peace among ourselves and with all nations.

ABRAHAM LINCOLN
2nd Inaugural Address (March 4th, 1865)

*but it can never forget
what they did here.*

★ ★ ★ ★ ★

...And I hope & think that the War will Be Over By that Time. I think that the Election or Reelection of President Lincoln will Do much Toward the Closeing of the War...I think that Every man that Belongs to Co. A will Vote for Old Abe without a Doubt..But I must close For it is 8 oclock at night & the Drum is Beating for Roll Call & I must go...

NEWTON SCOTT
CO. A. 36TH IOWA
NOVEMBER 3, 1864

It is for us,
the living,

★ ★ ★ ★ ★

WHEN JOHNNY COMES MARCHING HOME

When Johnny comes marching home again,

    Hurrah! Hurrah!

We'll give him a hearty welcome then,

    Hurrah! Hurrah!

The men will cheer, the boys will shout.

The ladies they will all turn out.

Chorus:

    And we'll all feel gay,

When Johnny comes marching home.

The old church-bell will peal with joy,

    Hurrah! Hurrah!

To welcome home our darling boys

    Hurrah! Hurrah!

The village lads and lasses say

With roses they will strew the way.

PATRICK SARSFIELD GILMORE

*rather to be dedicated
to the great task
remaining before us;*

★ ★ ★ ★ ★

THE BONNIE BLUE FLAG

We are a band of brothers, and native to the soil,

Fighting for the property we gained by honest toil;

And when our rights where threatened, the cry rose near and far,

Hurrah for the Bonnie Blue Flag that bears a single star!

Chorus:

Hurrah! Hurrah! For Southern Rights, hurrah!

Hurrah! For the Bonnie Blue Flag that bears a single star!

As long as the Union was faithful to her trust,

Like friends and like brothers we were kind, we were just;

But now when Northern treachery attempts our rights to mar,

We hoist on high the Bonnie Blue Flag that bears a single star.

HARRY MACARTHY

that from these
honored dead,

★ ★ ★ ★ ★

ORIGINAL DIXIE

I wish I was in the land of cotton,

Old times dar am not forgotten;

Look away, look away, look away, Dixie Land.

In Dixie Land, whar I was born in,

Early on one frosty mornin',

Look away, look away, look away, Dixie Land.

Chorus:

Den I wish I was in Dixie,

Hooray! Hooray!

In Dixie Land I'll took my stand,

To lib and die in Dixie;

Away, away, away down South in Dixie;

Away, away, away down South in Dixie.

we take increased
devotion to that cause

Oppression! I have seen thee, face to face, Do hail thee and they hord of hirelings base:--

And met thy cruel eye and cloudy brow; I swear, while life-blood warms my throbbing veins,

But thy soul-withering glance I fear not now— Still to oppose and thwart, with heart and hand,

For dread to prouder feelings doth give place Thy brutalising sway—till Afric's chains

Of deep abhorrence! Scorning the disgrace Are burst, and Freedom rules the rescued land,—

Of slavish knees that at thy footstool bow, Tramping Oppression and his iron rod:

I also kneel—but with far other vow Such is the vow I take—SO HELP ME GOD!

WILLIAM LLOYD GARRISON, abolitionist and
publisher of The Liberator, Boston 1831.

*for which they gave the last
full measure of devotion;*

Headquarters Army N. Va.
April 9th 1865-

Lt. Gen. U. S. Grant
Comdg Armies U.S.

General:

I have received your letter of this date
containing the terms of surrender of the Army of
Northern Va., as proposed by you. As they are sub-
stantially the same as those expressed in your letter of
the 8th inst, they are accepted. I will proceed to designate
the proper Officers to carry the stipulations into effect

Very Respectfully
Your Obt Servt.
(Sgd) R. E. Lee
General

Official
T. S. Bowers
A. A. G.

that this Nation,
under God,

★ ★ ★ ★

THE CIVIL WAR

THIRTEENTH AMENDMENT

SECTION 1. Neither slavery nor involuntary servitude, except as a punishment for crime whereof the party shall have been duly convicted, shall exist within the United States, or any place subject to their jurisdiction.

(Ratified December 6, 1865)

FIFTEENTH AMENDMENT

SECTION 1. The right of Citizens of the United States to vote shall not be denied or abridged by the United States or by any State on account of race, color, or previous condition of servitude.

(Ratified July 9, 1868)

shall have a new birth of freedom;

★ ★ ★ ★ ★

PETITION FROM "COLORED CITIZENS OF NASHVILLE" TO THE
UNION CONVENTION OF TENNESSEE, NASHVILLE, JANUARY 9, 1865:

We the undersigned petitioners, American citizens of African descent, natives and residents of Tennessee, and devoted friends of the great National cause, do most respectfully ask a patient hearing of your honorable body in regard to matters deeply affecting the future condition of our unfortunate and long suffering race.

First of all, however, we would say that words are too weak to tell how profoundly grateful we are to the Federal Government for the good work of freedom which it is gradually carrying forward; and for the Emancipation Proclamation which has set free all the slaves in some of the rebellious States, as well as many of the slaves in Tennessee.

After two hundred years of bondage and suffering a returning sense of justice has awakened the great body of the American people to make amends for the unprovoked wrongs committed against us for over two hundred years.

Your petitioners would ask you to complete the work begun by the nation at large, and abolish the last vestige of slavery by the express words of your organic law.

Many masters in Tennessee whose slaves have left them, will certainly make every effort to bring them back to bondage after the reorganization of the State government, unless slavery be expressly abolished by the Constitution.

We hold that freedom is the natural right of all men, which they themselves have no more right to give or barter away, than they have to sell their honor, their wives, or their children....

This is a democracy—a government of the people. It should aim to make every man, without regard to the color of his skin, the amount of his wealth, or the character of his religious faith, feel personally interested in its welfare. Every man who lives under the Government should feel that it is his property, his treasure, the bulwark and defence of himself and his family, his pearl of great price, which he must preserve, protect, and defend faithfully at all times, on all occasions, in every possible manner....

Five score years ago, a great American, in whose symbolic shadow we stand, signed the Emancipation Proclamation. This momentous decree came as a great beacon light of hope to millions of Negro slaves who had been seared in the flames of withering injustice. It came as a joyous daybreak to end the long night of captivity.

But one hundred years later we must face the tragic fact that the Negro is still not free. One hundred years later, the life of the Negro is still sadly crippled by the manacles of segregation and the chains of discrimination. One hundred years later, the Negro lives on a lonely island of poverty in the midst of a vast ocean of material prosperity. One hundred years later, the Negro is still languishing in the corner of American society and finds himself an exile in his own land. So we have come here today to dramatize an appalling condition.

In a sense, we have come to our nation's capital to cash a check. When the architects of our republic wrote the magnificent words of the Constitution and the Declaration of Independence, they were signing a promissory note to which every American was to fall heir. This note was a promise that all men would be guaranteed the inalienable rights of life, liberty, and the pursuit of happiness.

MARTIN LUTHER KING, JR.'S "I Have a Dream" speech, 1963

One day in 1863, the members of the Virginia Peninsula's black community gathered to hear a prayer answered. They listened as the Emancipation Proclamation was read under the branches of a tree known today as the Emancipation Oak. Hampton University's first students studied in the shade of the Emancipation Oak, located on the University's campus. The majestic giant is designated by the National Geographic Society as one of the great trees of the world.

and that government
of the People

★ ★ ★ ★ ★

by the People and for the People shall not perish from the earth."

Abraham Lincoln

(Gettysburg Address, November 1863)

★ ★ ★ ★ ★